Warrior Women in American History

THE ROLE OF WOMEN IN THE AMERICAN REVOLUTION

Cavendish Square
New York

Hallie Murray

Published in 2020 by Cavendish Square Publishing, LLC

243 5th Avenue, Suite 136, New York, NY 10016

First Edition

Website: cavendishsq.com

Cataloging-in-Publication Data
Names: Murray, Hallie.
Title: The role of women in the American Revolution / Hallie Murray.
Description: New York : Cavendish Square Publishing, 2020. | Series: Warrior women in American history | Includes glossary and index.
Identifiers: ISBN 9781502655554 (pbk.) | ISBN 9781502655561 (library bound) | ISBN 9781502655578 (ebook)
Subjects: LCSH: Women–United States–History–18th century–Juvenile literature. | United States–History–Revolution, 1775-1783–Women–Juvenile literature. | United States–History–Revolution, 1775-1783–Participation, Female–Juvenile literature.
Classification: LCC E276.M87 2020 | DDC 973.3082 B–dc23

Printed in the United States of America

Portions of this book originally appeared in *Women Soldiers, Spies, and Patriots of the American Revolution* by Martha Kneib.

Photo Credits: Cover, p. 3 Derived from Museum of Fine Arts, Boston/Wikimedia Commons/File: Sybil Ludington's Statue.jpg/Public Domain Mark; pp. 8-9, 10-11 Everett Historical/Shutterstock.com; p. 15, 54 North Wind Picture Archives/Alamy Stock Photo; p. 18 John Parrot/Stocktrek Images/Getty Images; p. 20 Science History Images/Alamy Stock Photo; pp. 26, 84-85 Copyright © North Wind Picture Archives; pp. 30-31 Kean Collection/Archive Photos/Getty Images; p. 32 Jason O. Watson/historical-markers.org/Alamy Stock Photo; pp. 36, 46 Library of Congress Rare Book and Special Collections Division; p. 38 Bob Thomas/Popperfoto/Getty Images; p. 40 Science History Images/Alamy Stock Photo; pp. 42-43 Library of Congress Prints and Photographs Division; pp. 49, 57 Hulton Archive/Archive Photos/Getty Images; pp. 52, 60, 81 Stock Montage/Archive Photos/Getty Images; p. 63 Hulton Archive/Getty Images; p. 68 Charlibear7/Wikimedia Commons/File: Sybil Ludington's Statue.jpg/CC BY-SA 4.0; pp. 70-71 Sergey Kohl/Shutterstock.com; p. 74 Bettmann/Getty Images; p. 77 © AP Images.

Contents

Introduction

Though Great Britain was technically victorious in the French and Indian War, the conflict took a lot of resources, and Britain as a country was facing bankruptcy. Since the war had been fought in America, the British Parliament believed the best way to fix the debt would be to raise taxes primarily from the colonies. These increased taxes began with the Sugar Act and Currency Act in 1764, which faced little opposition. But when the Stamp Act was introduced in 1765, the British citizens living in America began to feel these new tax laws were unreasonably harsh.

The Stamp Act required that taxes be paid on all printed materials, including legal documents, newspapers, and even playing cards. The cost of the Stamp Act was not particularly high, but it was the straw that broke the camel's back. Since the colonists did not have an official representative in Parliament, many believed such taxes were a violation of their rights as English citizens not to be taxed without consent. As activist James Otis Jr. declared, "Taxation without representation is tyranny." People began to resent the British government's control over the colonies, and some began to consider breaking away from British control entirely.

Resentment toward the British government grew, and across the colonies, small groups of people began to rebel in small ways, vandalizing and even committing violence against British officials. There was so much resistance that the Stamp Act was actually repealed in 1766, just six months after it was officially enacted, but by then it was too late. Rebellion had taken hold of the hearts and minds of too many. New acts of Parliament like the Townshend Acts of 1767 and the Intolerable Acts of 1774 (the Quartering Act, the Quebec Act, the Massachusetts Government Act, the Administration of Justice Act, and the Boston Port Act) added insult to injury, and political and intellectual leaders in the colonies began to advocate for a revolution.

In September 1774, many of these leaders met in Philadelphia, Pennsylvania, in what became known as the First Continental Congress to discuss their grievances with Britain and figure out a course of action. They were meant to meet again in 1775, but before they could do so, violence broke out in Massachusetts. The Battles of Lexington and Concord, which took place on April 19, 1775, are considered the first battles of the Revolutionary War. By June 1776, most colonists were in favor of breaking away from Britain. On July 2, the Continental Congress officially voted for independence, and on July 4, they adopted the Declaration of Independence. It stated that the thirteen colonies were officially at war with Great Britain and considered themselves sovereign states.

The war continued over the next two years, with both sides making victories and suffering losses. In 1778, France allied with America to lend aid against England, and Britain began to face major difficulties at home in Europe and in British India. In October 1781, England

This political cartoon was published by Benjamin Franklin in 1754. The message—"join or die"—was used to urge the colonies to band together. It later became a symbol of freedom from British control.

lost a key battle at the Battle of Yorktown, when the British general Lord Charles Cornwallis surrendered to the American general George Washington and French leader Jean-Baptiste Donatien de Vimeur, comte de Rochambeau. This loss allowed the anti-war Whigs of Britain's Parliament to take control, and in early 1782 they voted to end fighting in the colonies. In September of 1783, all parties involved signed the Treaty of Paris, which officially recognized the United States of America as a sovereign country and ended the American Revolution.

Though the majority of the leaders during the American Revolution were men, women played key roles behind the scenes. At the time, men's and women's lives rarely overlapped. Men were responsible for plowing fields, harvesting, and conducting business dealings and financial transactions, while women were often relegated

George Washington accepts the surrender of Charles Cornwallis after the rebels won the Battle of Yorktown in October 1781.

to household chores and bearing and raising children. Some men advocated for husbands to involve their wives more in major decisions and to discuss things like finances as a couple, but few actually did so.

During the war, however, women began to take a larger role in running their households and engaging in politics and public discussions by necessity. One of the major methods of protest used very early in the Revolution was boycotting British goods, including wool, tea, and candles. In order to successfully boycott, the male leaders of the movement would need to involve the people who were usually in charge of purchasing these things for their families: women. Later in the war, women whose husbands were called on to fight suddenly found themselves in charge of running entire households, farms, or even businesses in place of their husbands. Now that they were in charge, these women had to learn how to conduct themselves just as well as men or risk losing their family's livelihood.

Staying home doing the tasks normally left to men was not enough for some women. After the men rode off to war, these women engaged in heroic efforts to help make America independent. Some disguised themselves as men and went to fight at the front, while others gathered information or fought British supporters and soldiers in their hometowns. Still others used their words to encourage the public to support the war effort. Women could be found working for America's independence in every aspect of life in the American Revolution.

1

A Soldier Named Robert

Throughout history, there have been stories about women who disguise themselves as men in order to fight in wars. The American Revolution was no exception. Unfortunately for historians, women who did succeed in enlisting as men often didn't admit it unless they were caught, because at the time the idea of women doing "men's work" was seen as shameful and ridiculous. If any women survived their time in the army without being found out, they likely kept it a secret, making it impossible to know exactly how many women might have fought alongside men for the cause.

However, one woman was not silent about her service. Deborah Sampson, who disguised herself as a man and enlisted in the army under the name "Robert Shurtleff," was proud and outspoken about her role in fighting for America's freedom. In 1802, twenty years after she'd been honorably discharged from the military, Sampson began giving talks about her time in the service. Though women wouldn't be allowed to serve in combat for another two centuries, Sampson's legacy helped set in motion a change in cultural attitudes about what roles women can and should be allowed to hold in the military.

A Childhood in Servitude

Sampson was the eldest child out of six children born in Plympton, Massachusetts, to Jonathan Sampson and Deborah Bradford Sampson. They were a poor couple who could not provide for their family. The situation worsened when Sampson's father left home for an expedition at sea and never returned. Sampson's mother was now so desperate that authorities removed the children from the home and placed them elsewhere. Deborah was separated from her siblings and placed in the care of a distant relative. Three years later, when her guardian died, she was placed in the home of a farmer living in Middleborough, Massachusetts. She was now ten years old and was expected to work as an indentured servant.

As a servant, Sampson could not go to school. She listened instead to the lessons of others and borrowed the books of neighboring children. By working independently, she eventually learned to read and write. When she was eighteen years old, Sampson was free of her indenture, and she left the farm to find work in nearby Bellingham. One of the first things she did was acquire an education. Within a few months, she had so greatly increased her knowledge that she was better educated than children who had attended school for years.

After hostilities broke out, Sampson enthusiastically supported the war effort and plotted how she might serve in the army to fight for her country. Sampson had managed to save twelve dollars from a job with the local school, and she used it to purchase the cloth she would need for

This statue of Deborah Sampson wearing a Continental Army uniform stands outside the public library in Sharon, Massachusetts.

her disguise. As she completed each piece, she hid it in a haystack. Upon finishing the uniform, she announced to everyone that she was leaving the area to seek better wages. Instead, Sampson went only as far as the woods of Bellingham so she could change into her disguise.

Enlisting in the Army

Once she decided to enlist, Sampson used the name "Timothy Thayer." But as she signed the enlistment papers, someone she knew spotted her and her deception was exposed. The recruiters were furious. They tore up Sampson's enlistment papers and shouted at her to go home and behave like a proper woman. They threatened to punish her severely if she tried to enlist again.

Sampson could not be frightened away by angry recruiters. In fact, her entire life had been one of hardship, so the prospect of serving in the army must have seemed more like an adventure than something potentially dangerous. Her friends described her as fearless. "It cannot be denied that this romantic girl exhibited something of the same spirit as Joan of Arc [who] felt herself inspired with resolution to go forth and do battle in her country's cause."[1]

Like Joan of Arc, the fifteenth-century woman who led troops against a British invasion of France in 1429, Sampson felt as if she had also been called to defend her country against the British. She could not be deterred, and in May 1782, she managed to enlist as "Robert Shurtleff" and was enrolled for the entire length of the war. She was a volunteer in the Fourth Massachusetts Regiment, led by Captain Nathan Thayer.

Posing as a Man

Because she had grown up doing heavy labor on a farm, Sampson was well suited to this life of pretense as a man. She was strong enough to pass for a teenage boy and could keep pace with the men of the company. She had no problems marching or firing her musket.

Sampson's first test came when the company men were given uniforms. Because hers did not fit, she simply took out needle and thread and altered it herself. When the company commander's wife commented that it was strange for a boy to know so much about sewing, Sampson responded quickly. She said that her mother had been a seamstress, and as she had no sisters, she had been required to learn sewing to help her mother with her work. The explanation worked, and no more questions were asked.

For more than a year, Sampson led the life of a soldier. She fought in battles and endured hardships so courageously that she was commended by other men in her company and by her officers. Although they sometimes teased her by calling her "Molly" due to her beardlessness, the soldiers assumed she was a teenage boy too young to shave.

Life in the army was tough, but Sampson was familiar with hunger and long cold nights without a blanket. She persevered as bravely as the rest of her troop. Although she was wounded several times, sources disagree on the number and placement of her injuries. She was said to have had a sword cut to the head and then, four months later, been hit by a bullet that went through her shoulder. Other sources insist it was her thigh that was hit and that

Soldiers of the Contintental Army wore blue uniforms when they had them. The British army, on the other hand, dressed in red, which is why rebels called British soldiers "redcoats."

Wet, Cold, and Hungry

Soldiers in the Revolutionary War were badly paid and poorly fed. Money from Congress came slowly or not at all. Because roads were often impassable due to rain or snow, supply wagons of food often could not get to hungry troops. Many soldiers did not have shoes or blankets. Private Joseph Plumb Martin, who wrote an account of his war experiences, described many instances in which he nearly froze to death on cold nights or suffered exposure due to sleeping outside in pouring rain. "I was faint," he wrote, "having slept but very little the preceding night, nor had I eaten a mouthful of victuals for more than twenty-four hours. I waddled on as well and as fast as I could."[2] America's military was poorly organized and woefully undersupplied, and many deserted. But many more stayed to fight for their new country,

she hid in the woods until it healed. Because she was hiding her identity, she sought no medical treatment.

The Discovery

More than a year after she enlisted, Sampson's company was in Philadelphia when she became sick with what was then called "brain fever." Many soldiers had fallen ill with the same symptoms, and many had died. At first, Sampson tried to hide her sickness. She did not want to be taken to the hospital where her secret identity would undoubtedly be exposed. Eventually, she grew so ill that she was carried to the hospital and left there. At the time of her arrival, her condition was considered hopeless. At that time, patients in such a grave state were not well attended.

Still disguised as a man and dressed in a soldier's uniform, Sampson (*right*) delivered a letter to General George Washington (*center*).

One day, the attending physician, Dr. Barnabas Binney, walked by and asked how the young man in the bed was progressing. He was told that the man had died. The doctor felt for a pulse and, finding one, tried to place his hand on the man's heart. When he did so, he discovered that his male patient was a woman with her breasts bound to her chest by bandages.

The doctor did not immediately reveal Sampson's secret. Instead, Sampson was given the best treatment the hospital could offer, and when she had recovered enough to be moved, the doctor took her into his own house. The doctor's niece was smitten by the brave young soldier. The doctor, however, did not tell his niece what he knew about the soldier called Robert Shurtleff. Fortunately, Sampson found a way to discourage the young girl's attraction without revealing herself.

An Honorable Ending

When Sampson had fully recovered from the fever, Dr. Binney went to her commanding officer. The commanding officer then ordered Sampson to carry a letter to General George Washington. She was by now certain her secret was out. Sampson delivered the order to Washington with trepidation, sure that she had been discovered and would be punished. But Washington, upon reading the letter, prepared an honorable discharge for her. He also gave her a small sum of money, enough to pay her expenses back home.

Sampson changed back into female attire and returned to Massachusetts. After the war ended, she married Benjamin Gannett in 1784, and they had three children: Earl, Mary, and Patience. Although she kept busy on the farm with her husband, Sampson also took the time to give lectures about her war experiences. After much protest in 1792, she was given back pay the army had previously withheld from her. By 1805, Congress voted that she should receive a war veteran's pension.

Today, there is a monument to Deborah Sampson in Plympton, Massachusetts, and another monument honors her in the nearby town of Sharon, where she is buried in Rock Ridge Cemetery.

2

Patriots with Pistols

Women didn't have to join up with the army to fight the British. Two famous stories from the American Revolution feature women who terrorized British soldiers and Loyalists through deception and daring. Sisters-in-law Rachel and Grace Martin borrowed their husbands' clothes and guns and surprised a British courier so thoroughly that he abandoned his assignment and turned right around, terrified of the young "men" who waved their pistols around with such abandon. Nancy Morgan Hart, on the other hand, needed no disguise to threaten the British and their supporters with her shooting skills, though it's said she did dress up as a man occasionally to spy on the British in their camps. Though they didn't officially enlist as Sampson did, these women all defied traditional ideas about femininity in order to support the cause of the American Revolution.

Threatening to Shoot the Messenger

The highly patriotic Elizabeth Martin was the mother of nine children, seven of whom were young men who served in the American army during the Revolution. Legend tells of a British officer who asked Martin how many sons she had, and when she answered that she had eight, seven in the Continental Army, he sneered and told her "Really, Madam, you have enough of them." Martin is said to have replied, "No, sir, I wish I had fifty."[1] The advice Elizabeth Martin gave her sons was passionate and patriotic: "Go, boys, fight for your country. Fight till death, if you must, but never let your country be dishonored. Were I a man, I would go with you."[2]

Rachel Martin and Grace Martin, the wives of Martin's two oldest sons, shared this strong patriotism with their mother-in-law. One night, they were given a chance to do their part for their country. While they were at home, they received information that a British courier, accompanied by two guards, would be coming along the road that night, carrying dispatches for British posts. Rachel and Grace devised a plan to capture the dispatches.

Both women changed into clothing taken from their husbands' closets, armed themselves, and then went to a point in the road where they knew the courier would pass. As the courier and his two guards approached their hiding spot, the two women jumped out of the darkness and aimed their pistols at the three men. Taken completely by surprise, the men immediately surrendered. Rachel and Grace took the dispatches from the courier and disappeared back into the darkness. Once they arrived home, they asked a trusted friend to take the messages to General Nathanael Greene.

The three men the women had waylaid now had no reason to continue on toward the British posts. They instead returned down the road, back past the Martin household. The men stopped there and asked for accommodations for the night. Elizabeth Martin asked them why they were back so soon after having passed the other way, and they replied they had been ambushed and relieved of their important papers by two young rebels. The three were accepted into the house, never knowing that they slept under the same roof as the "men" who had taken them prisoner.

"The Devil of a Wife"

Another famously passionate, gun-slinging, at-home hero was Nancy Morgan Hart. One of Georgia's most colorful patriots of the Revolutionary War, Hart was a six-foot-tall, cross-eyed, rather plain redhead with smallpox scars on her face who had a penchant for cursing.

Little is known of Hart's early life. Sources disagree on the year of her birth. Some historians say 1735, while others claim it to be either 1744 or 1747. Hart's birthplace is also unknown; it was probably either Pennsylvania or North Carolina. In the eighteenth century, people didn't necessarily keep records of the place and time of their birth unless they were from upper-class families. Nancy Morgan married Benjamin Hart sometime around 1755, and they moved to northern Georgia in 1771. There, Hart, a flame-haired sharpshooter, made an immediate impression on the locals, so much so that local Native Americans called the creek by her house "War Woman Creek."[3]

By the time the war broke out, Hart, who was described as "a honey of a patriot, but the devil of a wife," had eight children to raise.[4] Together with her husband, she helped farm more than 400 acres (160 hectares) in the Broad River settlement in Georgia. Despite the difficulty of raising eight children while acting as community midwife and pharmacist, Hart helped her husband with the farm and also hunted for wild game.

Women were central to certain parts of the war effort, including the push to boycott British goods. This image shows a housewife spinning wool in order to avoid buying cloth from England.

Hart thoroughly supported the fight for independence. Her husband, whom she described as a "poor stick," was less enthusiastic than she.[5] Hart was so zealous that she reportedly undertook dangerous tasks to help the patriot cause. According to various legends, she infiltrated British camps—sometimes acting like a half-wit, sometimes disguised as a man. She listened to the conversations and then reported back to patriot units. On one occasion, she went out with a basket of eggs to sell to the British and was so successful at eavesdropping that she was able to gather extremely valuable intelligence. By supporting the patriot cause and spying, Hart eventually became well known to British sympathizers in the area.

Avenging John Dooly

The event that propelled Hart from occasional spy to beloved heroine of colonial Georgia happened in Hart's own home. Her husband was working in the fields far away from the house, leaving Hart and their thirteen-year-old daughter Sukey alone at the little log cabin. Five or six Loyalists (sources disagree on a number) from the British camp in Augusta arrived at the cabin and demanded to be fed. They knew about the redheaded, loudmouthed woman who let everyone know how she felt about the British, and they wanted to make trouble for her.

At first, Hart adamantly refused to feed the men. She pointed out that she had only one turkey, and it was old. But the Loyalists were determined to give her as much trouble as possible. One of them shot the turkey and insisted again that Hart feed the men.

Although she was very angry, Hart began cooking. If the men were well fed they might go away without harming

The Tale of John Dooly

John Dooly was born in 1740 in South Carolina. In 1771, he became a land surveyor and developer, possibly following in the footsteps of his father-in-law. He became successful and eventually acquired land in Georgia as well as South Carolina. Early on, Dooly was against the Revolution, but he slowly came around, like Georgia residents, when he realized the possibility for social and economic growth in the colony if it were free from British rule. Dooly became a recruiter, a militia colonel, and soon a war hero. When the British retreated to the coast, Dooly and his supporters began to target Loyalists, arresting many and even executing some. As the war continued, the rebels' luck began to run out. Dooly had made many enemies, and on August 6, 1780, Dooly was allegedly murdered in his home by vengeful Loyalists.

her or Sukey. But as their dinner was being prepared, they began bragging about how they had just killed Colonel John Dooly in his bed. Dooly was a friend and neighbor of Hart's, and she was outraged by this act of violence. At that point, her plan changed from simply feeding the men and hoping they would go away to plotting their capture and death.

The Standoff

Hart began setting out the food and drink. She made sure the Loyalists had plenty of whiskey and entertained them with humorous stories. On the pretext of needing more spring water, she sent her daughter out of the house to raise the alarm. Hart and her neighbors had hidden a conch shell by the well and had arranged for everyone to know how to blow a signal if an emergency arose. Sukey fetched the water, but she also blew the conch shell and alerted her father and their neighbors to the situation at home.

When Sukey returned, Hart began passing the men's muskets outside to her through a hole in the log cabin wall. She had gotten three muskets outside the house before the men noticed what she was doing. They immediately rushed at her, but Hart picked up one of the muskets and pointed it at the men, who stopped.

This standoff continued for a few moments until one of the men reached for a gun. Hart shot him, dropped the single-shot weapon, and grabbed another musket that Sukey had passed back into the house. A second man moved, and Hart shot him as well. The first man died immediately, but the second was merely injured.

At this point, Benjamin Hart arrived with the neighbors to find his wife holding off the remaining Loyalists with another musket. Hart explained that these were the men who had killed Colonel Dooly. As revenge, the Harts and their neighbors killed the Loyalists by hanging.

Hart's Legacy

After the war, the Hart family moved to Brunswick, Georgia, where Benjamin Hart died. Later, Nancy Hart moved to Kentucky with one of her children, where she died in 1830. For her courage and resourcefulness, Hart became one of Georgia's most famous heroines. Hart County was named for her, as were the Nancy Hart Highway and the Nancy Hart Historical Park. Two memorials to her deeds have been erected in Hartwell, Georgia. In 1997, she was honored as a Georgia Woman of Achievement.

This woodcut shows Hart, with a child hiding behind her skirt, brandishing a gun and threatening three terrified Loyalists. Two other British supporters lie dead or injured on the floor.

Hart County was created on December 7, 1853, and named after Georgia's rebel heroine, Nancy Hart, and her husband, Benjamin.

In 1912, six well-preserved skeletons were unearthed within half a mile (0.8 kilometers) of the site of the Hart cabin. It cannot be proved, but many people believe these are the remains of the Loyalists who killed Colonel Dooly and then made the mistake of getting on the wrong side of Nancy Morgan Hart.

3

The Accidental Spy

Soon after its founding in the mid-1600s, the religious sect known as the Quakers, an offshoot of the Church of England, was largely forced to leave Britain because of religious persecution. Yet when Quakers arrived in America, they found themselves at odds with the Puritans of the Massachusetts Bay Colony. In the 1660s, many Quakers migrated south and west, settling in Rhode Island, New Jersey, and Pennsylvania.

By the 1700s, Quakers were a well-established religious community in America. When the American Revolution began, many Quakers supported the rebels privately, but they had trouble acting on their views because a key part of being Quaker is practicing pacifism and working to view all humans as friends and equals. In order to support the Revolution without compromising their beliefs, some Quakers resorted to other methods of fighting against British rule that didn't involve actual fighting. One of these was Lydia Barrington Darragh, who took information she'd overheard British soldiers discussing in her kitchen to a rebel army lieutenant. In doing so, she became a spy for the American cause, though she didn't set out to do so.

Staying Out of the Conflict

Lydia Darragh, née Barrington, was born in Dublin, Ireland, in 1729. In 1753, she married William Darragh,

Practicing Quakerism

Quakers are members of the religious movement formally known as the Society of Friends, which was founded during the English Civil War in the mid-1600s by George Fox. Quakers believe that everyone's relationship with God is very personal. They practice pacifism and advocate for equality and social justice. Today, there are even nontheist Quakers who participate in Quaker practices but don't necessarily believe in God. Quakers in American history have participated in causes for social justice. In the eighteenth and nineteenth centuries, most Quakers were abolitionists, and some worked to help escaped slaves on the Underground Railroad. During World War I and World War II, many Quakers were conscientious objectors, meaning they refused to participate in the military side of the war effort, preferring instead to focus on causes that would help further peace and unity.

a teacher, and shortly thereafter, the couple moved across the sea to Philadelphia. They lived with the large Quaker community there. Because her husband made very little money as a teacher, Lydia Darragh brought in most of the family's income through her various jobs as a nurse, midwife, and undertaker. The couple had nine children, though only four survived.

During the early days of the war, Darragh was not involved with the war effort. To do so would be to put herself at risk of being dismissed from the Quakers for breaking their tenets. Still, she supported independence. The British were aware of her feelings, but knowing her religion, they were not threatened by her. Darragh

General William Howe was a British officer who served as commander in chief of the British military in North America from September 1775 to May 1778.

herself would tell them, "Though we consider thee as a public enemy, we regard thee as a private friend. While we detest the cause thee fights for, we wish well to thy personal interest and safety."[1]

Home Invasion

In December 1777, Darragh found herself involved in the war despite her best efforts to remain out of the conflict. Her house was across the street from a building being used by General William Howe as his headquarters, and she was often visited by a British officer, Major John André. The major explained that Darragh's house would also be used by the British for private conferences.

Darragh had no choice but to let the British use the large back parlor of her home for their meetings. Darragh was told that a room in her house would be required that very evening and that she should prepare it for a meeting. Also, she was told that her family should go to sleep early so that they would not overhear anything that was discussed.

Darragh did as she was told. She prepared the room and sent her family to bed. She admitted the British into the house and assured them that everyone there was in bed except herself and that she would go directly there as soon as she had shown the officers to their meeting room.

However, Darragh was in a quandary. While she had publicly supported the patriot cause, she had never acted on her beliefs. Still, her family was so committed to the cause of independence that Darragh's son Charles was serving in the Second Pennsylvania Regiment at Whitemarsh, even though his actions now separated him from the religion in which he had been raised.

William Penn was an English nobleman and Quaker who founded the colony of Pennsylvania. In fact, "Pennsylvania" comes from the Latin for "Penn's woods."

Friends, Not Enemies

A fundamental tenet of Quakerism is pacifism—the belief that violence is never justified. Quakers therefore bar members from engaging in acts of war or violence for any reason. This policy of pacifism is echoed in their official declaration:

> We feel bound explicitly to avow our unshaken persuasion that all war is utterly incompatible with the plain precepts of our divine Lord and Law-giver, and the whole spirit of His Gospel, and that no plea of necessity or policy, however urgent or peculiar, can avail to release either individuals or nations from the paramount allegiance which they owe to Him who hath said, "Love your enemies."[2]

The allure of a religion that preached tolerance, equality, and peace was undeniable. Many Quakers left Britain for the colonies, including William Penn, who founded the colony of Pennsylvania as a place where Quakers would be free from persecution.

Darragh and her husband are not known to have objected to his service, though it must have pained them to see their son cast off his religion.

Darragh was not sure what she alone should do to support the war effort and protect her son's life. Her religion forbade her from becoming involved, but many soldiers' lives were at risk, including her son's. After a short time of nervous debate and a great deal of prayer, she got up, crept down the corridor, and eavesdropped on the British meeting.

Lydia Darragh tells an officer of the Continental Army the secret plans she overheard British officers discussing.

What Darragh Heard

At first, the murmurs of the men speaking were too quiet for her to hear through the door. Perhaps she even thought of going back to her bed. But soon a stronger voice spoke out, reading an order for troops to march from Philadelphia on December 4, 1777, in order to ambush General George Washington's forces at Valley Forge and Whitemarsh.

Darragh went back to bed. Soon she heard someone knocking on her door, but she did not answer. The person knocked a second time, more loudly, but still Darragh lay in bed without answering. Finally, after the third knock, this one very loud, Darragh rose and answered the door. She escorted Major André and the others out of her house and went back to bed, but did not sleep.

During her sleepless night, Darragh formulated a plan to warn Washington's troops. She was required to get a pass to leave the city, but she knew a way she could acquire one that would not raise suspicion. Early on the morning of December 3, Darragh went to Howe's headquarters and requested permission to get flour at a mill in the town of Frankford. Her request was not an unusual one and was granted as a matter of course.

Darragh took an empty flour sack and walked several miles through the snow until she found a member of the Pennsylvania militia. He was Lieutenant Colonel Thomas Craig, a friend of the family. She passed on the information she had heard and was assured by Craig that he would get the news to General Washington immediately. Darragh made him promise not to reveal who had given him the news, as the British would punish her and her family if they found out she had shared the information. Craig promised and left for Washington's headquarters.

Major John André was a British army officer who was caught by the Americans in 1780 and executed as a spy for working with the traitor Benedict Arnold. This sketch shows André's capture.

PLAN OF WEST POINT
PASSPORT
B Arnold
DESCRIPTION OF DEFENCES, ORDNANCE. WEST POINT
STATEMENT OF ORCES

Darragh then went to get the flour and returned home as if nothing unusual had happened.

A Hidden Contribution

Darragh was in a state of agitation as the British left Philadelphia for their planned ambush. But because of her warning, Washington was aware of the attack, and it was foiled. Darragh learned of this when Major André returned to question her about her family and whether any of them were awake the night of the meeting. Darragh insisted she had sent everyone to bed early. Major André was said to have replied, "You, Lydia, I know, were asleep; I had to knock on your door three times before you heard me. Yet it is certain we were betrayed. I am altogether at a loss to conceive who could have given information of our intended attack to General Washington."[3]

The officer left, and Darragh breathed a sigh of relief. Craig kept his word, and during the war, no one ever knew what Darragh had done. Her daughter Ann, however, told the story of her mother's courage years after the war was over and the danger had passed. Lydia Darragh died in Philadelphia at sixty years of age in 1789.

Writing Toward Revolution

Though America's freedom from Britain was largely won through blood and war, the written word also played a major role in the success of the Revolution. One of the most famous examples of this is the pamphlet *Common Sense* by philosopher Thomas Paine, which offered a new argument for American independence. Over five hundred thousand copies of the pamphlet were produced, and people across the colonies read and discussed Paine's ideas. Though women were surely part of some of these discussions, in general their opinions were not taken as seriously as men's. It would be highly unusual for a woman to speak out or write publicly about her opinions on the Revolution, but that's just what writer Mercy Otis Warren did.

During the war and after, Warren kept up a correspondence with many major political leaders, and she wrote several satirical plays that served as propaganda against the British government. After America gained independence, Warren wrote a well-circulated pamphlet that argued for the inclusion of a Bill of Rights in the new American Constitution. Warren also wrote one of the earliest histories of the Revolutionary War, *A History of the*

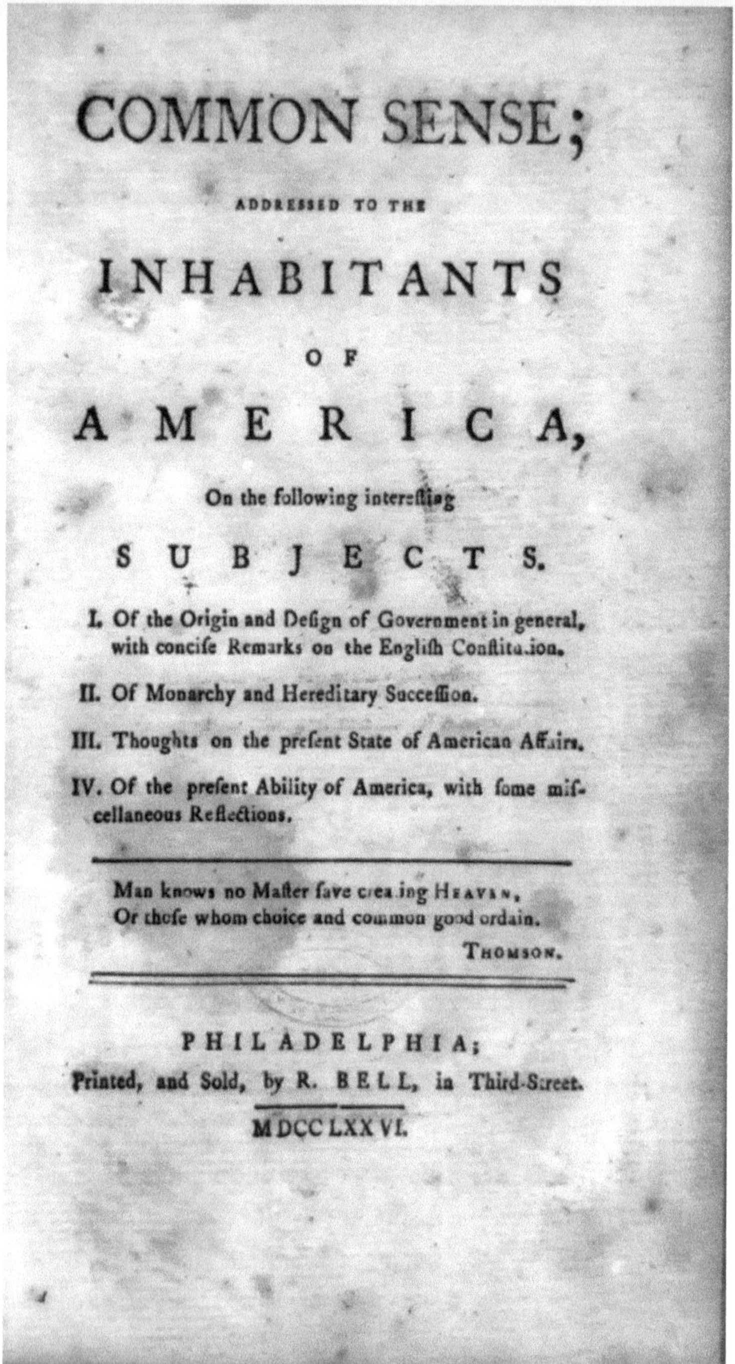

COMMON SENSE;

ADDRESSED TO THE

INHABITANTS

OF

AMERICA,

On the following interesting

SUBJECTS.

I. Of the Origin and Design of Government in general, with concise Remarks on the English Constitution.

II. Of Monarchy and Hereditary Succession.

III. Thoughts on the present State of American Affairs.

IV. Of the present Ability of America, with some miscellaneous Reflections.

Man knows no Master save creating HEAVEN,
Or those whom choice and common good ordain.

THOMSON.

PHILADELPHIA;
Printed, and Sold, by R. BELL, in Third-Street.

MDCCLXXVI.

Published anonymously in January 1776, *Common Sense* rapidly spread throughout the colonies and made a convincing argument for the fight for American independence.

Rise, Progress, and Termination of the American Revolution, which was published in 1805.

Growing Up in a Political Family

Mercy Otis Warren was born on September 25, 1728, in Barnstable, Massachusetts, to an upper-class family. Her family had come to the colonies in 1630 and had lived in the Plymouth area ever since. Warren herself never left the area of eastern Massachusetts, but through her plays and her correspondence, she was one of the more influential women's voices during the Revolution.

The Otis family was involved in politics, and Mercy listened with interest to the conversations between her father and her brother James. While her brothers were sent to Harvard, she, like other women of her time, was limited to the education she was able to obtain for herself, although her parents did encourage her to read extensively. Still, she was bitterly resentful that she was relegated to performing hours upon hours of needlework while the men in the family learned Latin and Greek and engaged in public discourse on political events.

The men in her family did not limit their involvement in the Revolution to mere debate on the issues, however. Mercy's brother James was so eager to spread the fever of independence that he had quarreled with a British officer in 1769 and received a brutal blow to his head. After that, he experienced occasional bouts of illness until his death in 1783, though he continued to espouse the patriot cause and served in the war.

At twenty-six years of age, Mercy Otis married James Warren, who was also avidly interested in politics. He

The Activism of James Otis Jr.

Mercy Otis Warren's older brother, James Jr., was also an activist and a revolutionary. He was a lawyer who got involved in the rebel cause after arguing a case against "writs of assistance," which allowed British officials to enter American homes without reason or notice. He later wrote many pamphlets that helped increase support for the Revolution, and he is perhaps best known for the phrase "taxation without representation is tyranny." Otis was also known for his belief that everyone was equal, including women, and he was a champion of gender and racial equality before those ideas were common or popular. It seems likely that Otis's beliefs about women's rights influenced his sister, Mercy Otis Warren, and empowered her to become a prolific writer despite the fact that women at the time were not encouraged to write or speak out about politics. Otis died in 1783 after being struck by lightning.

encouraged his wife's active involvement and supported her in her efforts. The Warrens eventually had five sons.

An Unsuitable Profession

Warren's political interests inspired her to turn to writing. In the years before the Revolutionary War, she wrote several plays: *The Adulateur* (1772), *The Defeat* (1773), and *The Group* (1775). In her plays, she skewered the British overlords of the colonies with her finely tuned sarcastic wit. The governor of Massachusetts, for example, was portrayed as Rapatio, a monster intent on raping the colony for the crown.

Warren was not afraid to direct her attacks at well-known public officials, though in the beginning her works

James Otis Jr., pictured here in a sketch dated circa 1770, was a lawyer whose impassioned legal arguments for American independence became key to the intellectual reasoning behind the Revolution.

were published anonymously. In puritanical New England, the job of playwright was considered a vulgar occupation, hardly fit for a man and certainly not for a woman. Acting in and writing plays was frowned upon throughout the colonies. The theater was not held in high repute as a cultural institution until well into the nineteenth century. Writing anonymously ensured that Warren's work would be read and not dismissed outright because of her gender.

However, Warren could not completely escape the influences of the culture in which she had grown up. Even though she had great talent and the support of her family, she still had nagging doubts about performing such unfeminine tasks. Her correspondence shows she often solicited the advice of friends on whether she was living her life appropriately. In a letter to John Adams, she asked if he would think her "deficient" in womanly attributes if she parodied Thomas Hutchinson, the governor of Massachusetts and a supporter of the Stamp Act, along with his political allies, in a new play. At the time, Adams supported Warren's desire to embrace the patriot cause through her plays and pamphlets, although in later years, when he himself was the subject of her sarcastic wit, he altered his opinion on the suitability of female writers.

The War in Letters

The ambiguity surrounding a woman who was a wife and mother as well as a political activist was represented by Warren's own husband, who referred to her as having a "masculine genius."[1] In other words, while he supported her efforts, he still felt her choice of vocation was unique within the realm of what was then considered acceptable feminine behavior.

Warren's husband served as a soldier during the war and often wrote descriptions of the battles he witnessed in his letters to his wife. In describing the Battle of Bunker Hill, in a letter dated June 18, 1775, he wrote, "It is Impossible to describe the Confusion in this place, Women & Children flying into the Country, armed Men Going to the field, and wounded Men returning from there fill the Streets. I shant Attempt a description—your Brother borrowed a Gun [and] went among the flying Bullets."[2]

Besides keeping informed of what was happening in the war, Warren supported the cause through her writing. She wrote to those people she knew were suffering due to the consequences of the war—not just her friends and acquaintances, but to anyone. When Warren learned of the death of General Richard Montgomery in January 1776, she wrote to his widow:

> While you are deriving comfort from the Highest Source, it may still brighten the clouded moment to reflect that the number of your friends is not confined to the narrow limits of the province but by the happy union of the American Colonies ... and the urn of the companion of your heart will be sprinkled with the tears of thousands who revere the commander at the gates of Quebec, though not personally acquainted with the General.[3]

Warren maintained correspondence with many of the important political figures of her day, including Samuel Adams, John Adams, and Thomas Jefferson. She was also a lifelong correspondent of John Adams's wife, Abigail. Abigail Adams once wrote to Warren:

One of Warren's many high-powered correspondents was Thomas Jefferson, a lawyer and intellectual who would go on to serve as America's third president from 1801 to 1809.

> You, Madam, are so sincere a lover of your country, and so hearty a mourner in all her misfortunes, that it will greatly aggravate your anxiety to hear how much she is now oppressed and insulted. To you, who has so thoroughly looked through the deeds of men, no action, however base or sordid, no measure, however cruel and villainous, will be a matter for any surprise.[4]

To Warren, who wrote of the plight of the colonies with such passion, her opinions and actions were not heroic, but instinctive. She wrote:

> The late convulsions are only the natural struggle which ensued when the genius of liberty arises to assert her rights in opposition to the ghost of tyranny. I doubt not this fell form will ere long be driven from our land. Then may the western skies behold virtue, which is generally the attendant of freedom. Seated on the throne of peace, where may she ever preside over the rising commonwealth of America.[5]

A Mighty Pen

Oppression in the American colonies was not the only political issue addressed in Warren's works. In her play *The Group*, she argued that women should have the right to be liberated from abusive husbands. Later, in a nineteen-page pamphlet, she opposed the ratification of the US Constitution because it did not yet have a bill of rights, it did not provide term limits for elected officials, and

This statue of Mercy Otis Warren can be found near the Barnstable County Courthouse in Warren's hometown of Barnstable, Massachusetts.

it provided no safeguard against the federal government raising a standing army.

During the war, Warren began a history of the Revolution, which eventually became a work entitled *A History of the Rise, Progress, and Termination of the American Revolution.* It was published in 1805 when Warren was seventy-seven years old. Warren was no longer satisfied with being anonymous; her three-volume history was published with her name proudly displayed upon it.

Because of this, Warren is often considered the first true American woman author. Other women were writing at the same time, and a few others were published, but normally women did not expect their work to find publication. Warren was the first woman in the country who wrote with the goal of having her work published and distributed widely.

Mercy Otis Warren died in 1814. In her honor, a bronze statue was dedicated at the courthouse in Barnstable, Massachusetts, on July 4, 2001. It stands opposite a statue of another Barnstable patriot hero, her brother James Otis Jr.

5

Raising Money for the War Effort

Though she was born and raised in England, Esther DeBerdt Reed was a staunch supporter of the American Revolution. She had only lived in America for five years when the war began, but she soon became a key figure in the relief effort at home, as she took a lead in organizing fund-raising through the Ladies Association of Philadelphia.

Reed strongly believed that women could and should actively engage in the war effort, and she publicly argued that to refuse to do so was in fact unpatriotic. Reed inspired women across the colonies to help raise money and express their support for the rebel cause. She unfortunately passed away in 1780 and was unable to see the effects of her ardent patriotism, but her legacy lived on in the hearts and minds of the many women who became involved in the war effort because of Reed's actions.

The British Merchant's Daughter

Esther DeBerdt Reed was born in London in 1746, the only daughter of Dennis DeBerdt, a successful merchant whose main business was with the American colonies. Due to the nature of DeBerdt's pursuits, many of his American clients and business partners visited the DeBerdt residence

Dated circa 1760, this image shows Esther DeBerdt Reed as a proper young woman, befitting her station as a wealthy merchant's daughter.

in London. One of them, Joseph Reed, wooed the young Esther. Eventually, they were engaged.

However, Esther's father disapproved of the match, at least until such time as Joseph Reed had established himself in business. By 1765, Reed had returned to Philadelphia to begin his quest for a stable career and income. At first, his law practice went well, but when business eventually deteriorated, the engagement of Esther and Joseph stretched for five long years.

Esther, though raised to be politically loyal to Great Britain, had been exposed to too many ideas from the colonies to quietly accept that they should tamely submit to British domination. She wrote in one letter that she detested Prime Minister George Grenville and member of Parliament Alexander Wedderburn because "they are such enemies to America."[1] In 1769, Joseph Reed returned to Great Britain to find his fiancée's family beset by bankruptcy and grief over Dennis DeBerdt's death. The young couple were married in May 1770. In October of that same year, Joseph Reed returned to Philadelphia with his British bride.

A Family in Motion

When the war broke out, Joseph joined the army, leaving his wife at home to work the farm and raise their two children. Reed's letters also show that at this time, she was a little unsure how to conduct herself while her husband was away. She wrote to Joseph in 1777, "As I am not famous for making good Bargains in things out of my Sphere I shall put it off as long as possible, in hopes you may be at home before it is too late."[2] However, like many other women in the colonies, Reed learned to manage without a spouse and thus became much more self-reliant and confident in her abilities.

Several times during the war, Reed was forced to move her family to escape the approach of British forces. They moved first to Burlington, Vermont, and then to Evesham, New Jersey, where an aged relative and a female friend joined Reed and her children while Reed struggled with poor health due to the recent birth of her third child. The family later moved to Flemington, New Jersey, where they remained until after the British withdrawal from Philadelphia in 1778.

One of Reed's children died of smallpox that year, and she wrote, "Calamity has over come me, and struck the very bottom of my heart."[3] Shortly thereafter, the family returned to their home in Philadelphia. Joseph Reed had been elected governor of the state, and the family enjoyed high status and acclaim for both Reed's endurance of hardship and her husband's new position.

In 1780, Reed gave birth to another child, a son named George Washington Reed. Although ill again from the effects of childbirth, Reed gallantly contributed her time and effort to a new project that she initiated: the Ladies Association.

Involving Women in the War

On June 10, 1780, thirty-three-year-old Reed published a pamphlet entitled *The Sentiments of an American Woman.* In the pamphlet, she declared that American women would not be content to simply wait at home for the men to determine the outcome of the war.

Because getting women actively engaged in the war effort meant deliberately crossing gender lines, Reed

Martha Washington, pictured here circa 1790, was the wife of George Washington, the first president of the United States.

composed her arguments in such a way that women's involvement would seem patriotic rather than scandalous. She listed famous heroines of the past, like Joan of Arc, who had fought "the ancestors of these same British, whose odious yoke we have just shaken off, and whom it is necessary that we drive from this Continent."[4]

Reed admitted in the pamphlet that there would be those who disapproved of her endeavors, but she insisted that a true patriot would "applaud our efforts for the relief of the armies which defend our lives, our possessions, our liberty."[5] By depicting those who would bar women's involvement in the war as unpatriotic, Reed won many sympathizers. Only three days after the publication of the pamphlet, thirty-six Philadelphia women met to decide how they could best focus their efforts.

The group was to begin a fund raiser. The women were determined to send all contributions to Martha Washington for direct disbursement to the troops. The plan required an enormous amount of organization because the women wanted to cover all thirteen colonies. Their plan called for each colony's efforts to be supervised by a "Treasuress" and for these women in turn to be supervised by the wife of the governor of that colony. Reed, as the wife of Pennsylvania's governor, was responsible for approaching the wives of the other governors.

Canvassing with the Ladies Association

The Philadelphia group immediately set out by dividing the city into ten equal districts and assigning women to canvass each district. The women traveled in pairs and were instructed to visit every house without exception. Many prominent women of the day participated in the

The Maid of Orléans

Joan of Arc was born to a peasant family in France around 1412, during the Hundred Years' War, the 1337–1453 fight between the Plantagenets of England and the French House of Valois for control over France. Joan of Arc believed that God had chosen her to help France win the war, and she convinced the prince of Valois to let her lead his army in battle against the English at the city of Orléans. The Valois army won, and people began to believe Joan of Arc was the prophesied "virgin who would save France." In 1430, however, she was captured by the English and accused of witchcraft, and on May 30, 1431, she was burned at the stake. Many viewed her as a martyr, and she has since become an extremely popular symbol of feminine patriotism and bravery. In 1920, she became a saint of the Catholic Church.

canvassing, including Sarah Franklin Bache, the daughter of Benjamin Franklin.

Normally, women of such social standing at that time would not dream of soliciting people of all classes, including strangers, and asking them for contributions. But the women approached the canvassing with the fervor associated with their zeal for independence. One of the participants wrote anonymously, "Those who were in the country returned without delay to the city to fulfil their duty."[6]

The women were received well by most people, but less well by some. The anonymous letter writer continued, "As the cause of their visit was known, they were received with all the respect due to so honorable a commission."[7] On the other hand, Anne Rawle's description of the women is less

Women participating in wars throughout history have viewed Joan of Arc as a hero and model of patriotic femininity.

complimentary: "Of all absurdities the Ladies going about for money exceeded everything."[8] Rawle was writing her mother, Rebecca Shoemaker, whose second husband was an exiled British sympathizer. She continued, "I fancy they raised a considerable sum by this extorted contribution."[9]

Overall, the Ladies Association canvassers were greeted warmly, and many people contributed to their cause. By early July, the women had collected more than $300,000 in continental dollars. (Due to inflation, this was worth only about $7,500 in gold.) Still, it was a worthy sum, and the women were duly proud of their efforts.

Converting Silver to Shirts

The distribution of the money collected by the Ladies Association was hampered not by the citizens of Philadelphia but rather by George Washington himself. The general felt the money should not be disbursed directly to the troops, allegedly because he was nervous that soldiers would simply use the money for things like alcohol instead of much-needed supplies. He told the Ladies Association that the soldiers were in need of linen shirts.

Reed, disappointed that Washington had taken their successful effort and translated it into mere women's work, like sewing, wrote Washington again asking for permission to send cash to the soldiers. Washington again refused her request. Reed's husband wrote her, "The General is so decided that you have no Choice left so that the sooner you finish the Business the better."[10]

Reed realized she would have to fulfill Washington's request or all the efforts of the association would be wasted. The Philadelphia Ladies Association made more than two thousand shirts, each embroidered with the name of the woman who made it. Unfortunately, Reed did not live to see the project to completion. She died that fall of dysentery, which was sweeping through Philadelphia. The administration of the Ladies Association fell to Sarah Franklin Bache.

The women were thanked by George Washington when their work was completed. With the relegation of such ardent supporters of independence to the level of mere seamstresses, the Ladies Association and the funding drive begun by Reed has, somewhat unfairly, been characterized by some historians as "George Washington's Sewing Circle." Yet more groups soon took up the call thanks to Esther DeBerdt Reed's idea, and several other colonies formed organizations that contributed greatly to the war effort.

6

The Messenger and the Military Wife

One of William Shakespeare's most famous lines is from *Twelfth Night*: "Some are born great, some achieve greatness, and some have greatness thrust upon them." During the Revolutionary War, women were not called on as often as men to perform "great" things, but they often did anyway. Sybil Ludington and Margaret Corbin were two women who had greatness "thrust upon them," when men—in Ludington's case, a messenger, and in Corbin's, a cannon rammer—were injured or killed. In these times of need, Ludington and Corbin stepped up, filling traditionally male roles when there was no one else to do so.

The British Are Coming!

"The British are burning Danbury—muster at Ludington's!"[1]

Two years after Paul Revere's famous midnight ride, a sixteen-year-old farm girl rode 40 miles (64 km) through the night to alert the militia of Fredericksburg, New York (present-day Ludingtonville), to danger.

Born in 1761 to Colonel Henry Ludington, a well-known and respected militia officer, and his wife, Abigail, Sybil Ludington was the oldest of twelve children. As with other girls who had younger siblings, most of Ludington's time was spent doing household chores and caring for her brothers and sisters when her mother was occupied with her own tasks.

Sybil Ludington was just putting the younger children to bed on the night of April 26, 1777, when a messenger reached the family's home with the news that the British were burning the town of Danbury, Connecticut, 17 miles (27 km) away. The messenger had come from Danbury's militia with a request for aid from Fredericksburg. The Danbury militia's food stores and munitions had been destroyed by the British, and the militia needed men, ammunition, food, and supplies to continue the fight.

Sybil Saves the Day

Unfortunately, all the men of the Fredericksburg militia had temporarily been relieved of duty that day so they could see to the spring planting on their farms, meaning it would be difficult to assemble them quickly. Yet everyone would have to be alerted if aid was to be sent to Danbury. Colonel Ludington himself could not sound the alarm, as he had to remain at his house to supervise the muster.

The messenger from Danbury couldn't go either; not only was he exhausted from his journey, but he was unfamiliar with the Fredericksburg area. He would not be able to find each farmhouse that would need to be alerted. Sybil Ludington, however, knew where the militiamen who had the responsibility of warning their area if danger arose

This statue of Sybil Ludington can be found outside the public library in Danbury, Connecticut, whose burning prompted her historic ride.

lived. Ludington needed only to visit these houses for the word to then spread to everyone in the community.

Ludington was eager to volunteer. Even though it was dark and raining, she had no doubt that she could find her way. Her father reluctantly agreed to let her go. After warning her to beware of British soldiers as well as "skinners," Henry Ludington sent his daughter off. Skinners were lawless men who used the chaos surrounding the war to make themselves rich by stealing. They had no allegiance to either the American or British side, although sometimes they dressed in uniforms as a disguise.

Ludington promised her father she would be careful. She departed her home around 9 p.m. and traveled nearly 40 miles (64 km). She rode far and wide throughout the county, from the town of Kent, south to Mahopac, and north to Stormville, telling the men of the area of the need in Danbury. By the time Ludington and her horse returned home at dawn, wet and exhausted, nearly four hundred men had departed to Danbury to fight the British.

Some Loss, Some Gain

Danbury lay in ruins; the Fredericksburg militia was organized too late to save it. But the militia was able to engage the British at the Battle of Ridgefield the following day on April 27, stopping the British advance. Before they could reach Putnam County, New York, where the Ludingtons lived, the British retreated from Ridgefield and went back to their ships, which were anchored in Long Island Sound. Ludington's bravery may not have saved Danbury, but it did result in the British halting their advance through New England.

In 1975, for the bicentennial of the American Revolution, a series of stamps was created to celebrate "Contributors to the Cause." This stamp honors Ludington, a "Youthful Heroine."

U.S.
8c
Youthful Heroine

After the war, Ludington married Edmond Ogden, and the couple settled in the town of Catskill. Ludington had one son, Henry. Her husband died when Henry was only thirteen years old, so Ludington was forced to raise Henry alone. She supported herself and her child by working as a tavern keeper. Henry eventually became a lawyer, and his son graduated from West Point and became a military hero in his own right. There is a monument dedicated to him at Fort Riley in Kansas.

Sybil Ludington died in 1839 at her son's home in Unadilla, New York. Today, there is a trail dedicated to Ludington's route through Putnam County, New York. It is designated by markers for those who wish to retrace the path the sixteen-year-old took during the night of April 26, 1777. Ludington's ride was also commemorated on a US postage stamp in 1975.

The War Wife

Margaret Cochran Corbin was born in November 1751, near Chambersburg, Pennsylvania. At the age of five, her parents were killed, and relatives raised Margaret and her siblings. In 1772, Margaret married John Corbin. When he enlisted in the First Company of Pennsylvania Artillery, Margaret refused to be left behind.

As was the case with many war wives, she had nothing to stay behind for, and so she became what is known as a camp follower. During the American Revolution, camp followers were the wives of the soldiers who followed the army and performed services like cooking food, laundering clothing, mending clothes, and tending to the wounded.

Corbin made herself popular with the men in her husband's battery, and they began to call her "Molly."

Corbin used the nickname "Molly" for the rest of her life, and is sometimes thought to be Molly Pitcher—a famous female hero of the Revolution who many historians believe might have been Mary McCauley and who had a story that was similar to Corbin's.

Fetching water wasn't the only thing Corbin did—along with the other tasks she handled at the camp, she learned how to clean and load a cannon from the soldiers of her husband's regiment.

(Wo)Manning the Cannon

In November 1776, the British occupied New York City. The Continental Army largely fled the city, leaving two thousand Pennsylvania, Virginia, and Maryland men at Fort Washington on Manhattan Island, one of them being John Corbin. George Washington felt the fort should

Grueling Conditions

Life for camp followers like Corbin was difficult. Just like the soldiers, they lived in very poor conditions through hot summers and freezing winters. They were not strangers to hunger and exhaustion. While recognizing that the women performed labor essential to the survival of the army, the army commanders had a tendency to dismiss them as a nuisance. The women received only a half-ration of the food allotted to the men. In one case, though, the laundresses of General Anthony Wayne's regiment held a strike until they were guaranteed better pay and living conditions. But even slightly improved circumstances could not keep the life of the camp followers from being hard and miserable.

Molly Pitcher, also known as Mary McCauley, loads a cannon at the Battle of Monmouth. That nickname is sometimes associated with Corbin too.

be completely evacuated, but General Nathanael Greene argued that it should be defended. Washington eventually agreed to this, and supplies and ammunition were ferried across the river to the fort.

On November 16, the defenders of the fort were attacked by Hessian infantry. Hessians were professional soldiers from Germany who had been hired by the British to help them in the war. During the battle, John Corbin was struck and killed by enemy fire. Margaret ran to him, but there was nothing she could do. Immediately, she picked up the rammer, the stick used to ram a cannonball to the bottom of the barrel. By doing this, she performed the task that had been her husband's duty.

Soon, Corbin herself was struck by enemy fire. She was wounded in the shoulder and jaw, and her left arm was almost severed from her body. She lay with the rest of the wounded and dead on the battlefield.

The Bloody Aftermath

The Hessians killed many of the wounded after the battle, but for some reason, they did not kill Corbin. Perhaps the soldier who first found her thought she was dead, or perhaps he did not want to bayonet a woman. Eventually, the British took Corbin prisoner. But within a short time, they had handed her over to the Continental Army.

Corbin was stuck in a straw-filled cart with others who were wounded during battle and taken to Philadelphia. The trip must have been excruciatingly painful. It seems unlikely that anyone could have survived injuries such as Corbin's without bleeding to death or dying of infection, but somehow she survived.

In June 1777, Congress approved the formation of the Invalid Regiment, which was composed of soldiers too disabled to fight again. Corbin was enrolled in the regiment and remained on its rolls until it was disbanded in 1783.

In 1779, Corbin was awarded $30 by the state of Pennsylvania, "to relieve her present necessities due to her disabled condition caused by wounds received while she filled with distinguished bravery the post of her husband who was killed by her side serving a piece of artillery at Fort Washington."[2] Congress voted her a military pension of half her husband's pay for the rest of her life. This was the first time a woman had been granted a military pension by the United States.

Honoring Captain Molly

Life did not get easier for Corbin or the people around her after the war. She never regained the use of her arm and could not work, and records indicate that she was unable to bathe or dress herself. She also had habits like smoking, drinking, and swearing, as well as a terrible temper. The ladies of the area snubbed Corbin due to her uncouth ways, so she spent most of her time at the local garrison, trading stories with the soldiers. Because she had so little money, the soldiers offered her their cast-off clothing, which meant Corbin could usually be found dressed as an artillery officer. She persuaded everyone to call her Captain Molly and even convinced the soldiers to salute her.

Corbin had caregivers who used her pension for her upkeep. But Congress was often slow in paying the money, which made her caretakers cross. In 1795, Quartermaster William Price complained, "I am at a loss what to do with

This monument marks what was believed to be Corbin's grave at the United States Military Academy, but in 2017, it was discovered that the remains inside are actually those of a man.

Capt. Molly. She is such an offensive person that people are unwilling to take her in charge."[3]

Corbin died in 1800 at the age of forty-nine. She was originally buried above the Hudson River near Highland Falls, New York, but in 1926, the Daughters of the American Revolution located her overgrown grave and arranged for her reburial at West Point. She was reinterred with full military honors, a granite memorial, and a bronze plaque. Or at least that's what was believed.

In October 2017, the grave that was thought to hold Corbin was disturbed by construction, and the body was removed. Tests revealed that the skeleton actually belonged to a male who had likely lived during the 1800s, a century later than Corbin. The Daughters of the American Revolution have since worked to uncover more about their hero, Captain Molly, but it's tough to find any evidence, especially because Corbin has no living descendants. She lives on in legend, though the location of her bones remains a mystery.

7

The Legacy of Women's Involvement

During the American Revolution, women not only made valuable contributions to the war effort, as demonstrated in these pages, but also showed that they could handle tasks at home and in their communities that had formerly been performed by men. Throughout American history, the large demand for men to fight as soldiers and serve in other military positions during wartime has created space for women to expand their roles beyond the domestic sphere. Progress isn't linear, but historically women have made large cultural strides in the wake of large-scale conflict. Women's contributions during World War I, for instance, were leveraged as a major argument for giving women the right to vote, which was finally granted in 1920 with the Nineteenth Amendment.

Finding a Voice

As wars have done across the centuries, the American Revolution motivated many people, especially women, to push for cultural change. Though women gained the right to vote after World War I, the fight for that right began before America was even a country. In 1776, Abigail Adams wrote to her husband, "If perticular care and attention is not paid to the Ladies, we are determined to foment a Rebelion, and will not hold ourselves bound by any Laws in which we have no voice, or Representation."[1] Abigail Adams was determined to push the boundaries of what was considered acceptable behavior for women at the time. She was realistic enough, though, to acknowledge that things wouldn't change in her own lifetime.

The end of the war did not vastly improve the situation for colonial women, but some strides had been made. Women who had learned to run farms and businesses while the men were away fighting were not eager to return to merely doing housework and taking care of children. For women who had married the men their parents chose for them, especially for those who were unhappily married, forcing their daughters into arranged unions was no longer acceptable. Women who had gained an education through hard work and dogged determination were not inclined to allow their own daughters to grow up illiterate.

Shifting Family Dynamics

But it was not just the women who had changed. Some men's opinions about women had changed, too. For example, a New Englander, William Palfrey, once dismissed his wife's opinions and advice. Palfrey thought of his wife, Susan, as an extension of himself. When, in 1778, she wanted to move to Boston, a decision he opposed, he chided her in a letter, "Can you suppose that I can possibly have an Interest separate from yours?" He insisted that when it came to his family's best interests, "You cannot possibly

Abigail Adams was a writer and the wife of the second president of the United States, John Adams.

be a Judge."[2] This condescending tone had changed only a year later after his wife had competently taken over the family's financial affairs. Palfrey began regularly consulting with his wife on financial matters, and before he sailed to France on a diplomatic mission, he informed his wife of all the arrangements he had made concerning his estate.

Timothy Pickering also learned the value of a wife who was educated in conducting the family business. In June 1777, he sent a lame horse home, instructing his wife to ask his male friends for advice on how to care for it, saying such a task was "entirely out of [your] sphere."[3] His letters continued in this tone for several years, but eventually Pickering changed his tune. While he was off fighting the war, his wife capably handled their farm, rented another farm, supervised the building of their new home, and got the harvest in, all while caring for a newborn infant. Pickering wrote in 1783, "This war which has so often [and] long separated us, has taught me how to value you."[4]

Lucy Knox wrote to her husband, a prominent Continental officer, that when he came home from the war, "I hope you will not consider yourself as commander in chief of your own house—but be convinced ... that there is such a thing as equal command."[5]

Women in Public

In love as well as business, things had changed on the home front. Young girls who had seen their mothers overcome obstacles to become successful in business and farming were not necessarily interested in either marrying young or in what their parents had to say about their choice of husband. The adults who had fought the war agreed with the sentiment. Thomas Jefferson declared in a letter to a French acquaintance in 1790, "According to the usage of my country, I scrupulously suppressed my wishes, that my daughter might indulge her own sentiments freely."[6] An anonymous New Englander declared in 1784, "In a matter of such importance, a young woman ought to [be] left [e]ntirely to herself."[7]

Even the previously dreaded title of spinster was no longer as spurned as it had been. Instead, women began to realize the value of choosing a life according to their own wishes, whether or not that meant marriage. Spinsterhood came to be seen by some as "a situation that may be supported with great dignity."[8]

The Right to Learn

Perhaps the biggest change to society after the Revolution was in the matter of education. Before the war, most women received no education, except perhaps some instruction on reading the Bible. If a girl wanted more schooling, she generally had to find a way to get it on her own. After the war, public schools were opened to girls as well as boys. Private academies also began admitting female students. In these schools, girls learned history, geography, and mathematics alongside the boys. The early nineteenth century saw many female reformers emerge from this first generation of educated American women. The women of past generations encouraged their relatives and friends to take advantage of these newfound opportunities. Abigail Adams wrote to a niece in 1785, "It is from feeling the disadvantages of it myself, that I am the more solicitous that my young acquaintance should excel me."[9]

In this image, a patriot serves tea to a British officer in order to get information out of him. Because of social expectations, women were often underestimated by the men around them, which some used to their advantage.

C.S. REINHART-'96

In 1800, Eliza Southgate of Maine remarked, "I do not esteem marriage absolutely essential to happiness."[10]

While it is true that some marriages became more egalitarian compared to before the war, by and large the situation for women remained little improved. The main change had come in the form of people's altered perception of what constituted the "female sphere." Raising children was still considered the highest feminine calling, but women's options would never again be as restricted as they had been.

The Long Fight for Equality

The heroines of the Revolutionary War did more than simply perform one or two courageous feats. Deborah Sampson may have had to dress as a man to fight for her country, but eventually women would be able to serve in the armed forces without the need for disguise. Mercy Otis Warren may have felt forced to publish her plays anonymously for fear of attracting derision for entering an occupation intended only for men, but by the early nineteenth century, Warren and other women were putting their own names on their written work.

The war didn't change everything, but it did open a few doors for women. The woman who was supposed to be happy staying in the home, raising children, and being innocent of finances or farm work had become more knowledgeable, skilled, and independent. In 1798, Judith Sargent rather colorfully predicted that women had entered a new dawn of history. She said that women were "emerging from the clouds which have hitherto enveloped them, and the revolution of events is advancing in that half of the human species, which hath hitherto been involved in the night of darkness."[11]

Women had a long way to go, but heroines like Deborah Sampson, Lydia Darragh, Mercy Otis Warren, Margaret Cochran Corbin, Nancy Morgan Hart, and countless others braved scorn, derision, and sometimes death to take the first few steps in a new direction for women in the United States.

Chronology

1763 The French and Indian War ends with the signing of the Treaty of Paris, also known as the Treaty of 1763.

1764 British Parliament passes the Sugar Act and the Currency Act.

1765 Parliament passes the Stamp Act.

1766 Due to widespread indignation, the Stamp Act is repealed.

1772 Mercy Otis Warren's *The Adulateur* is published.

1773 Mercy Otis Warren's *The Defeat* is published.

Margaret Cochran Corbin marries John Corbin.

The Boston Tea Party, a protest against a tax on tea, occurs when a number of rebels board ships in Boston Harbor and dump their cargo overboard.

1774 The First Continental Congress meets in Philadelphia, Pennsylvania.

1775 Mercy Otis Warren's *The Group* is published.

The Battles of Lexington and Concord mark the beginning of the Revolutionary War.

The Battle of Bunker Hill is fought outside Boston.

1776 Thomas Paine's *Common Sense* is published.

The colonies declare their independence from England with the Declaration of Independence.

Margaret Cochran Corbin is wounded in the Battle of Fort Washington.

1777 Sybil Ludington rides to muster the militia.

The Invalid Regiment is formed, and Margaret Corbin is enrolled.

The British capture Philadelphia and occupy New York City.

Lydia Darragh delivers secret information to the American army.

1778 France enters the Revolution on the side of the United States.

The British Army withdraws from Philadelphia.

1779 Margaret Corbin is awarded a military pension.

1780 Esther DeBerdt Reed begins her fund-raising campaign and publishes *The Sentiments of an American Woman*. She passes away the same year.

John Dooly is murdered in his home by Loyalists.

1781 General Cornwallis surrenders at Yorktown, Virginia, losing a key battle for the British.

A plan for a temporary form of government for the Unites States called the Articles of Confederation is ratified.

1782 Deborah Sampson enlists under the name Robert Shurtleff.

1783 The Treaty of Paris, which officially ends the war, is ratified by Congress.

1805 Congress grants Deborah Sampson a veteran's pension.

Mercy Otis Warren's three-volume history of the Revolutionary War is published.

Chapter Notes

Chapter 1
A Soldier Named Robert

1. Lincoln Diamant, editor, *Revolutionary Women in the War for American Independence: A One-Volume Revised Edition of Elizabeth Ellet's 1848 Landmark Series* (Westport, CT: Praeger Press, 1998), p. 35.
2. Joseph Plumb Martin, *A Narrative of a Revolutionary Soldier* (New York: Signet Classic, 2001), p. 33.

Chapter 2
Patriots with Pistols

1. Lincoln Diamant, editor, *Revolutionary Women in the War for American Independence: A One-Volume Revised Edition of Elizabeth Ellet's 1848 Landmark Series* (Westport, CT: Praeger Press, 1998), p. 174.
2. Diamant, p. 174.
3. Patricia Edwards Clyne, *Patriots in Petticoats* (New York: Dodd, Mead & Company, 1976), p. 43.
4. Diamant, p.190.
5. Diamant, p.188.

Chapter 3
The Accidental Spy

1. Lydia Darragh, quoted in Pamela Kline and Paul Pavao, "Lydia Darragh: Quaker, Pacifist, and American Spy," Revolutionary-War.net, https://www.revolutionary-war.net/lydia-darragh.html (accessed April 24, 2019).
2. "The Position of the Society of Friends with Regard to War," Quaker.org, http://quaker.org/legacy/

mounttoby/statements/historical%20statements.html (accessed April 24, 2019).

3. Lincoln Diamant, editor, *Revolutionary Women in the War for American Independence: A One-Volume Revised Edition of Elizabeth Ellet's 1848 Landmark Series* (Westport, CT: Praeger Press, 1998), p. 115.

Chapter 4

Writing Toward Revolution

1. Mary Beth Norton, *Liberty's Daughters 1750–1800* (Ithaca, NY: Cornell University Press, 1980), p. 121.
2. James Warren, "Letter from James Warren to Mercy Otis Warren," Massachusetts Historical Society, http://www.masshist.org/bh/warrenp1text.html (accessed April 24, 2019).
3. Lincoln Diamant, editor, *Revolutionary Women in the War for American Independence: A One-Volume Revised Edition of Elizabeth Ellet's 1848 Landmark Series* (Westport, CT: Praeger Press, 1998), p. 47.
4. Diamant, p. 44.
5. Diamant, p. 46.

Chapter 5

Raising Money for the War Effort

1. Lincoln Diamant, editor, *Revolutionary Women in the War for American Independence: A One-Volume Revised Edition of Elizabeth Ellet's 1848 Landmark Series* (Westport, CT: Praeger Press, 1998), p. 96.
2. Mary Beth Norton, *Liberty's Daughters 1750–1800* (Ithaca, NY: Cornell University Press, 1980), p. 216.
3. Diamant, p. 98.
4. Norton, p. 179.
5. Norton, p. 179.
6. Norton, p. 180.

7. Norton, p. 180.
8. Norton, p. 180.
9. Norton, p. 180.
10. Norton, p. 186.

Chapter 6

The Messenger and the Military Wife

1. Susan Campbell, "An Unheralded Patriot Girl," *Hartford Courant*, May 30, 2005, https://www.courant.com/news/connecticut/hc-xpm-2005-05-30-0505300421-story.html.
2. Margery Pepiot, "Captain Molly," National Muzzle Loading Rifle Association, https://www.muzzleblasts.com/archives/vol3no4/articles/mbo34-3.shtml (accessed April 24, 2019).
3. Pepiot, "Captain Molly."

Chapter 7

The Legacy of Women's Involvement

1. Mary Beth Norton, *Liberty's Daughters 1750–1800* (Ithaca, NY: Cornell University Press, 1980), p. 226.
2. Norton, p. 220.
3. Norton, p. 221.
4. Norton, p. 222.
5. Norton, p. 224.
6. Norton, p. 229.
7. Norton, p. 229.
8. Norton, p. 240.
9. Norton, p. 263.
10. Norton, p. 242.
11. Norton, p. 295.

Glossary

ambush A trap in which a concealed person lies in wait in order to attack another person by surprise.

bankruptcy The state of being impoverished.

boycott To purposefully refuse to have dealings with a person, store, or organization; to refuse the traded goods of a foreign country or countries.

canvasser A person who goes door-to-door throughout a district in order to raise money, solicit political support, or determine opinions.

deserted Abandoned or left without permission or the intention to return.

disbursement A payment from a specific fund.

Hessian A German soldier paid by the British to fight for them during the American Revolution.

indentured servant A servant who is bound to a master for a specific number of years, after which he or she is free to work elsewhere.

Loyalist An American who was loyal to the British cause; also called a Tory.

martyr A person who sacrifices himself or herself for a cause or who is killed for his or her beliefs.

militia Local men who would gather when called to fight but were not enlisted in the army.

pension A fixed sum paid regularly to a person following his or her retirement from service.

Quartering Act A law that required the colonies to provide housing and supplies to British troops.

skinner A thief who was not allied with either British or American forces.

surveyor A person whose job is to measure a specific amount of land, like a person's property.

tenet Core belief.

Bibliography

"Amazing Women in War and Peace." Userpages.aug.com. Accessed April 25, 2019. http://userpages.aug.com/captbarb/femvets.html.

Bailyn, Bernard. *The Ideological Origins of the American Revolution*. Cambridge, MA: Belknap Press, 1992.

Bois, Danuta. "Margaret Cochran Corbin." Distinguished Women of Past and Present. Accessed April 30, 2019. http://www.distinguishedwomen.com/biographies/corbin.html.

Campbell, Susan. "An Unheralded Patriot Girl." *Hartford Courant*, May 30, 2005. https://www.courant.com/news/connecticut/hc-xpm-2005-05-30-0505300421-story.html.

Clyne, Patricia Edwards. *Patriots in Petticoats*. New York: Dodd, Mead & Company, 1976.

Commager, Henry Steele, and Richard B. Morris, eds. *The Spirit of Seventy-Six: The Story of the American Revolution as Told by the Participants*. New York: De Capo Press, 1995.

Dacquino, V. T. "Sybil Ludington: The Call to Arms." Catskill.net. Accessed April 25, 2019. http://www.catskill.net/purple/sybil.htm.

DePauw, Linda Grant. *Founding Mothers: Women in America in the Revolutionary Era*. Boston: Houghton Mifflin Company, 1975.

Diamant, Lincoln, ed. *Revolutionary Women in the War for American Independence: A One-Volume Revised Edition of Elizabeth Ellet's 1848 Landmark Series.* Westport, CT: Praeger Press, 1998.

Garraty, John A., and Mark C. Carnes, eds. *American National Biography.* New York: Oxford University Press, 1999.

"Grace and Rachel Martin." Women in the American Revolution. Accessed April 25, 2019. http://rims.k12.ca.us/women_american_revolution/martin.html.

Gunderson, Joan R. *To Be Useful to the World: Women in Revolutionary America, 1740–1790.* New York: Twayne Publishers, 1996.

Hintzen, William. "Betty Zane, Lydia Boggs, and Molly Scott: The Gunpowder Exploits at Fort Henry." WVCulture.org. Accessed April 25, 2019. http://www.wvculture.org/hiStory/journal_wvh/wvh55-4.html.

Hoffman, Ronald, ed. *Women in the Age of the American Revolution.* Perspectives on the American Revolution. Charlottesville, VA: University of Virginia Press, 1989.

"The Intolerable Acts." USHistory.org. Accessed April 25, 2019. http://www.ushistory.org/us/9g.asp.

James, Edward T., Janet Wilson James, and Paul S. Boyer, eds. *Notable American Women, 1607–1950: A Biographical Dictionary.* Cambridge, MA: Belknap Press of Harvard University Press, 1971.

Kline, Pamela, and Paul Pavao, "Lydia Darragh: Quaker, Pacifist, and American Spy," Revolutionary-War.net,

April 24, 2019. https://www.revolutionary-war.net/lydia-darragh.html.

"Lydia Darragh." USHistory.org. Accessed April 30, 2019. http://www.ushistory.org/people/darragh.htm.

"Lydia Darragh." Women in the American Revolution. Accessed April 25, 2019. http://rims.k12.ca.us/women_american_revolution/darragh.html.

Maier, Pauline. *From Resistance to Revolution: Colonial Radicals and the Development of American Opposition to Britain, 1765–1776*. New York: Alfred A. Knopf, 1973.

Martin, Joseph Plumb. *A Narrative of a Revolutionary Soldier*. New York: Signet Classic, 2001.

Michals, Debra. "Nancy Hart." National Women's History Museum. Accessed April 29, 2019. https://www.womenshistory.org/education-resources/biographies/nancy-morgan-hart.

Michals, Debra. "Sybil Ludington." National Women's History Museum. Accessed April 29, 2019. https://www.womenshistory.org/education-resources/biographies/sybil-ludington.

"Nancy Morgan Hart." Georgia Women of Achievement. Accessed April 29, 2019. https://www.georgiawomen.org/nancy-morgan-hart.

Norton, Mary Beth. *Liberty's Daughters: The Revolutionary Experience of American Women, 1750–1800*. Ithaca, NY: Cornell University Press, 1980.

Pepiot, Margery. "Captain Molly." National Muzzle Loading Rifle Association, April 24, 2019. https://www.muzzleblasts.com/archives/vol3no4/articles/mbo34-3.shtml.

"The Position of the Society of Friends with Regard to War." Quaker.org. Accessed April 24, 2019. http://quaker.org/legacy/mounttoby/statements/historical%20statements.html.

Powell, Jim. "William Penn, America's First Great Champion for Liberty and Peace." Quaker.org. Accessed April 29, 2019. http://www.quaker.org/wmpenn.html.

"Sybil Ludington." Historic Patterson, New York. Accessed April 29, 2019. http://www.pattersonny.org/SybilLudington.htm.

Warren, James. "Letter from James Warren to Mercy Otis Warren." Massachusetts Historical Society. Accessed April 25, 2019. http://www.masshist.org/bh/warrenp1text.html.

The White House. "Esther DeBerdt Reed." Accessed April 25, 2019. http://www.whitehouse.gov/kids/dreamteam/estherreed.html.

Zeinert, Karen. *Those Remarkable Women of the American Revolution*. Brookfield, CT: Millbrook Press, 1996.

Further Reading

Books

Alberti, Enigma. *Anna Strong and the Revolutionary War Culper Spy Ring*. New York, NY: Workman Publishing Company, 2019.

Casey, Susan. *Women Heroes of the American Revolution: 20 Stories of Espionage, Sabotage, Defiance, and Rescue*. Chicago, IL: Chicago Review Press, 2015.

Meltzer, Brad. *The First Conspiracy: Young Reader's Edition*. New York, NY: Roaring Brook Press, 2020.

Staats, Ann McCallum. *Women Heroes of the US Army: Remarkable Soldiers from the American Revolution to Today*. Chicago, IL: Chicago Review Press, 2019.

Websites

American Battlefield Trust

www.battlefields.org

The American Battlefield Trust works to preserve battlefields around the country and has information and documents from a number of different battles and conflicts, including the American Revolution.

Daughters of the American Revolution

www.dar.org

The Daughters of the American Revolution is a national society of women descended from the men and women who fought for independence in the American Revolution. It works to preserve and uncover historical facts and artifacts.

National Women's History Museum

www.womenshistory.org

The website of the National Women's History Museum in Alexandria, Virginia, offers digitized exhibits, articles, and other resources about women throughout American history.

Index